PLEASURE S _____RS

Andrew Gladwell

SHIRE PUBLICATIONS

Published in Great Britain in 2013 by Shire Publications Ltd, Midland House, West Way, Botley, Oxford OX2 0PH, United Kingdom.

43-01 21st Street, Suite 220B, Long Island City, NY 11101, USA.

E-mail: shire@shirebooks.co.uk   www.shirebooks.co.uk

A CIP catalogue record for this book is available from the British Library.

Shire Library no. 711.   ISBN-13: 978 0 74781 205 0

Andrew Gladwell has asserted his right under the Copyright, Designs and Patents Act, 1988, to be identified as the author of this book.

Designed by Tony Truscott Designs, Sussex, UK and typeset in Perpetua and Gill Sans.

Printed in China through Worldprint Ltd.

13 14 15 16 17   10 9 8 7 6 5 4 3 2 1

COVER IMAGE
The paddle steamer *Waverley* is the last sea-going paddle steamer in the world. She now travels around the coastline of the UK to keep alive the tradition of British pleasure steamers.

TITLE PAGE IMAGE
Seaside resorts were the preferred destination for most passengers, but beauty spots such as Lulworth Cove were also popular. Passengers were landed there from paddle steamers such as the *Consul* in unique fashion along a plank directly on to the beach.

CONTENTS PAGE IMAGE
Queen of the North at Blackpool around 1920. Blackpool was a natural centre of cruising, with the Lake District, North Wales and the Isle of Man all being easily accessible by steamer.

ACKNOWLEDGEMENTS
I would like to thank the people who have allowed me to use illustrations, which are acknowledged as follows:

Alamy, front cover; Eric Close, page 10 (bottom); Corbis, pages 16 (bottom), 33, 34 and 41 (bottom); Tom Gilmore, pages 45 and 47; Andrew Gladwell, pages 3, 4, 5, 7, 9 (bottom), 10 (top), 14, 15 (bottom), 16 (bottom), 18 (top), 21, 26, 29, 30, 31 (top), 32 (top), 35, 36, 37, 40, 44 (top), 46 (top), 48, 54, 55 (top & bottom), 57, 58, 60 and 61; Guildhall Library, City of London/The Bridgeman Art Library, page 6 (bottom); Mary Evans Picture Library, pages 6 (top), 8 and 9 (top); Paddle Steamer Preservation Society, pages 1, 11, 16 (top), 17 (top), 18 (bottom), 19, 22, 23, 28, 31 (bottom), 32 (bottom), 38, 41 (top), 43 (top), 44 (bottom), 49, 50 (top), 51, 53 (top & bottom) and 56 (bottom); Phil Richardson, pages 12, 15 (top) and 52; Ron Warwick, pages 17 (bottom), 20 and 56 (top); and Paul Wymark, pages 24, 25, 42, 43 (bottom), 46 (bottom) and 50 (bottom).

Shire Publications is supporting the Woodland Trust, the UK's leading woodland conservation charity, by funding the dedication of trees.

CONTENTS

BEGINNINGS

PLEASURE STEAMERS tend to inspire a sense of nostalgia in people. In their heyday these happy little ships were an indispensable feature of the seaside as they plied between coastal piers and harbours. They enabled holidaymakers of all classes to enjoy a day or a few hours experiencing the glories of the British coastline, as well as providing fast and economical transport in the days before air travel and the mass use of cars.

The idea of paddle power to propel a ship goes back to Roman times but it was not until 1802, on the Forth & Clyde Canal, that the first paddle steamship, William Symington's *Charlotte Dundas*, appeared, and it was another ten years before the first commercially viable paddle steamer entered service. The wooden *Comet* began operation on the Clyde on 6 August 1812. *Comet* became the first paddle steamer to ply regularly with passengers in Europe. It measured only 40 feet by 10 feet and was constructed by John Wood of Port Glasgow with an engine made by John Robertson of Glasgow. Its maiden voyage from Port Glasgow to Glasgow, a distance of about 20 miles, took three and a half hours. *Comet* immediately caught the imagination of passengers, who were now able to travel far more quickly and in greater comfort than before. More paddle steamers were soon built, and services were extended to call at such places as Campbeltown and Largs, as well as sailings on inland lochs such as Loch Lomond. Soon after, the first paddle steamer named *Waverley* was built for Captain Robert Douglas by Lang of Dumbarton. It was placed in service on the Clyde between Glasgow and Helensburgh.

The *Comet* proved to be a great success and the design was soon copied at other major ports and cities around Britain. Over the following decade or so, as this novel form of steam propulsion

In 1812 *Comet* became the first commercially viable paddle steamer to operate in the British Isles. *Comet* was small and built of wood. Within little more than a decade, paddle steamers were to become a common sight around the coast and harbours of the United Kingdom.

WILLS'S
CIGARETTES.

"THE COMET."

4

was developed, a number of early steamer companies were established, and one of the first was the General Steam Navigation Company, formed in 1824. The River Thames was an obvious location for this innovation as London, as the capital city, was growing rapidly. By 1820 its population had reached 1.25 million, representing a large potential market of passengers eager to experience a river trip. There were a number of rival operators offering services, each loudly proclaiming the merits of its own steamers. Many early steamer passengers on the Thames were travelling to visit one of the exotic pleasure gardens that had been established by the river, one of the greatest of which was Rosherville, near Gravesend.

Steamers, however, were not confined to trips to pleasure gardens. The British seaside resort had its origins in the late eighteenth and early nineteenth centuries, and the growth of resorts was greatly stimulated by the coming of the railways in the 1830s and 1840s. Paddle-steamer routes were extended further afield to compete with the trains and similarly influenced the expansion of most of the seaside resorts that we know today. Many resorts had primitive, often wooden, piers at which paddle steamers could land their passengers. As the steamers became larger and the frequency of their services increased, so the piers were often rebuilt to meet new requirements. Although the railways were able to provide fast and often direct services, paddle steamers had an advantage in providing quick links between resorts and towns on either side of estuaries or between islands and the mainland.

Alongside the development of paddle steamers to serve the burgeoning seaside resorts went their use as ferries and working craft at ports such as Southampton, Liverpool, Glasgow and Bristol. Ferry services became available

Industry at the Broomielaw. An early paddle steamer built in 1814, *Industry* was made from oak from the Kilbirnie estate and had a folding funnel. Its distinctive grinding noise gave it the nickname of the 'Coffee Mill'.

An early
River Thames
paddle steamer
alongside the
Town Pier at
Gravesend. This
pier catered for
early visitors to
the nearby
Rosherville
Gardens.
It provided an
excellent place
for promenading
as well as joining
a steamer.

Early Thames
paddle steamers
between London
Bridge and
Southwark Bridge
around the 1820s.
Early paddle
steamers usually
had open decks
with no cover
for passengers in
inclement weather.
Another feature
was the tall
stove-pipe funnel.

to places such as the Isle of Wight and remote parts of the Firth of Clyde. Journeys that had formerly been long or treacherous were now easy, affordable and available to most people.

Inevitably, as services developed and technology and facilities advanced, passengers were conveyed further afield. Advances in the construction of piers by eminent specialist engineers such as Eugenius Birch enabled piers to

be extended further out to sea, allowing the new paddle steamers to land at all states of the tide. This permitted more places to be linked by paddle steamer and the potential for services was fully exploited. What had started as quite modest routes soon became extensive networks.

As services developed and as competition increased, steamers became larger and passenger accommodation improved. Most early paddle steamers were rather basic, with limited passenger facilities. Temporary bars and places to serve refreshments were often created by placing wooden trestle tables across barrel tops. This taught the steamer owners that profits could be made from food and drink as well as from fares. Bars and dining facilities developed in this period and the potential for making money from passengers captive on a steamer cruise was fully exploited with typical Victorian ingenuity.

On the Firth of Clyde, railway routes spread during the 1830s and 1840s. Paddle steamers soon enhanced the services provided by the railways to give fast crossings across the Firth, linking many islands and harbours that the railway alone could not reach. Paddle steamers and trains were timetabled to interconnect, and these excellent links guaranteed the success of both. The Firth of Clyde was a perfect location for operating paddle steamers. They were able to provide swift links between Glasgow, other large towns and ports and the growing seaside resorts favoured by the Victorian masses. Merchants and businessmen were also able to commute quickly between their offices and their pleasant new homes on picturesque lochs remote from the boisterous city. Mail and goods could now also be carried quickly and efficiently.

Most piers were built for paddle steamers. They were often rebuilt and enlarged to cater for bigger vessels and increasingly large fleets. This photograph shows massive berthing arms for disembarking passengers at all states of the tide.

Marian on Loch
Lomond around
1818. The first
paddle steamer
on the loch,
Marian was
likened to
an angry
whale, susprising
frigtened tourists
with its hissing
and roaring as it
circumnavigated
the lake with a
foamy wake.

Quite soon, the tradition of going 'doon the watter' was started. Glasgow had a long tradition of celebrating annual fairs, and 'Glasgow Fair' soon became synonymous with paddle steamers. Hordes of Glasgow folk would board the steamers at the Broomielaw or catch a steam train to the coast to link in with a steamer. The Firth of Clyde has an abundance of attractive harbours and bays, and numerous seaside resorts quickly developed along its shores, among them Rothesay, Largs, Dunoon and Ayr. Rothesay became the most popular resort, being so close to Glasgow and therefore reached quickly and cheaply from the city.

As well as the major tourist destinations, the Firth of Clyde also offered a number of smaller calling points, where a small pier would provide access to a village. Some holiday accommodation was available at these places but the main users of such piers were wealthy businessmen who built splendid villas along the shore. The village of Tighnabruich is a good example of this.

Thus by the mid-nineteenth century most of the industrial regions of Britain were linked with resorts and coastal towns further afield by paddle steamer. By this time, what were to become the main pleasure-steamer cruising areas of the United Kingdom had developed: the River Thames, the Firth of Clyde, the Bristol Channel, North Wales, and the south coast – all areas with one or more large cities positioned around 60–80 miles from somewhere that passengers might want to visit, perhaps to view the scenery, to visit friends, to conduct business, or just to enjoy themselves. Those wanting to escape everyday life for a day at the coast provided a ready-made market for steamer operators. What better way was there to escape from the city than by one of the ever larger and more magnificent paddle steamers?

On the south coast two principal companies came to dominate paddle-steamer services: Red Funnel and Cosens. Cosens was formed at Weymouth in 1852, initially to operate services between Weymouth and

Passengers
aboard a Firth
of Clyde steamer
around the 1880s.
At this time,
seaside resorts
were being
developed and
paddle steamers
provided the best
way of getting
to places such as
Rothesay, Dunoon
and Largs.

The Firth of
Clyde's most
developed and
popular port of
call was Rothesay.
The large pier
was always a
hive of activity as
steamers arrived
and departed. The
Glasgow tradition
of going 'doon the
watter' started in
the mid-Victorian
era.

9

The Firth of Clyde
had many small
piers that served
villages and small
settlements.

Comet at
Weymouth.
A paddle tug
built of wood, it
operated on the
Swanage to Poole
service, along with
Telegraph. Comet
was eventually
broken up
in 1906.

Portland. In the early years they experienced some competition, stimulating the introduction of new steamers. Early steamers included *Highland Maid* and *Prince*. A rival company, John Tizard, operated *Premier* in direct competition from Weymouth. Competition increased when Tizard introduced *Ocean Bride* and *Contractor*, but eventually, in 1876, John Tizard joined Cosens. Such keen competition was to a great extent beneficial to the

expansion and improvement of services as it ensured that competitors acquired new ships, increased passenger comfort and opened new routes, with only the best steamers and most popular routes surviving. This provided a firm foundation for the paddle-steamer services that would thrive in the late Victorian era.

One of the highlights of the mid-Victorian era for Cosens was the construction and entry into service of the *Empress*. Regal names became the norm for Cosens in subsequent years as *Monarch*, *Queen* and *Victoria* arrived. In this period Cosens introduced routes conveying passengers as far afield as the Channel Islands, Cherbourg and Torquay.

Empress entered service in 1879 for Cosens. It operated services from Weymouth to the Isle of Wight and Torquay. Its oscillating engines remarkably survive to this day.

The Isle of Wight played a significant part in the development of the paddle steamer. In 1861 the longest-named and longest-surviving steamer operator, the Isle of Wight & South of England Royal Mail Steam Packet Company (more commonly known as Red Funnel), commenced services between Southampton and the Isle of Wight, using piers such as those at Cowes, Ryde and Yarmouth. This was the heyday of the Isle of Wight as a fashionable resort, being frequently visited by Queen Victoria, whose holiday home was Osborne House near Cowes.

Any operator of paddle steamers at the time could never go wrong by giving its steamer a regal name, and so *Her Majesty*, *Princess Beatrice* and *Princess Helena* entered service on the south coast during the 1880s to cope with increasing trade and increased passenger expectations. The Red Funnel steamers between the Isle of Wight and the mainland experienced a relatively unchallenged early history.

By the later years of the Victorian era the paddle steamer had developed to the point where the facilities, atmosphere, layout and size remained more or less stable for the next decade or two.

Vectis entered Isle of Wight service in 1866 and was the first steamer to be custom built for Red Funnel.

THE NEW PALACE STEAMERS, Ltd.
P.S. "ROYAL SOVEREIGN" UNDER LONDON BRIDGE

VICTORIAN AND EDWARDIAN HEYDAY

BY THE 1880s, not only the design and facilities of the typical paddle steamer but also their main excursion areas had stabilised. The host of original operators had also to a great extent shrunk to the key main companies that would dominate services for the next eighty years. The British Empire was reaching its zenith, and such operators of paddle steamers as the General Steam Navigation Company, Cosens, P. & A. Campbell, Red Funnel and the Caledonian Steam Packet Company must have felt that the sun might never set on their own little empires.

The paddle steamers of the mid- and late Victorian period reflected the class-consciousness of the time. As in all aspects of life, passengers of each class were segregated as far as possible. For the affluent middle classes, first-class saloons were the norm. These were positioned in the most pleasant and roomiest areas of the steamer. Their decor imitated the nicest Victorian drawing rooms, with fine mahogany furniture, rich drapes, gilded fittings and richly upholstered couches. The lower classes were given more basic, wooden seating in the less salubrious areas of the steamer, often below the waterline.

Paddle steamers of all periods were propelled by two large wheels placed at the centre section of either side of the hull. The paddle wheel is a large wheel built on a steel framework. The frame had a number of floats (usually of timber) fitted upon the outer edge of the wheel. Sometimes these floats were adjusted, or 'feathered', to provide the maximum amount of push against the water. The bottom quarter or so of the wheel travelled underwater as it turned. Most British paddle steamers had solid drive shafts. These required both wheels to turn ahead or astern together. This limited the ship's manoeuvrability and gave a wide turning circle.

By the 1880s the Thames-based General Steam Navigation Company (GSNC) faced challenges typical of the era, in increased competition and a fleet that needed updating. In 1887 it took the brave decision to order no fewer than five new paddle steamers for their Thames services. With the arrival of the *Mavis*, *Oriole*, *Halcyon*, *Philomel* and *Laverock*, the GSNC achieved supremacy on the Thames services.

Opposite:
Royal Sovereign about to pass under London Bridge. Many pleasure steamers departed from the City of London. They had telescopic funnels to allow them to pass under the bridge. One of the last of these steamers was the *Crested Eagle*.

Ivanhoe cruising on the Firth of Clyde. Steamer operators initially felt threatened when the railways arrived. They soon realised that the railways could reach only so far and that steamers could take passengers to more remote places.

By this time, a regular network and timetable of services had developed on the Thames estuary, serving the great urban sprawl of London as well as the newly developed seaside resorts of Kent and Essex. In 1905 the first turbine steamer entered service when the *Kingfisher* replaced the *Halcyon*, although the GSNC never favoured turbine steamers, continuing to prefer paddle steamers. In 1909 one of the greatest and most fondly remembered Thames paddle steamers, *Golden Eagle*, entered service. With its fine uncluttered promenade deck, *Golden Eagle* soon became a great favourite on the London to Margate and Ramsgate run.

Passengers cruising aboard the *Ivanhoe* on Loch Long around 1910. The Firth of Clyde provided splendid scenery for cruising. Loch Goil and Loch Long were amongst the favourite locations.

S.S. "Lucy Ashton"

NORTH BRITISH RAILWAY SERIES

Among the most distinctive features of a paddle steamer are the paddle boxes. The massive paddle boxes and their foamy wake can be appreciated in this view of the Clyde's *Lucy Ashton*. Another notable feature of these steamers was the accessibility of the engines to view.

River Thames services were dominated by the General Steam Navigation Company from the 1820s until its demise in the late 1960s. Other operators challenged them, but they never stole the mantle of the GSNC as the main operator on the London river.

However, the long-established GSNC did encounter some competition with its services. One of the most majestic of all paddle steamers, *La Marguerite*, was operated by the Victoria Steamboat Association. At 1,554 tons it was the largest paddle steamer ever to operate on the Thames. Its large size was ultimately the cause of significant problems, as a large steamer would be profitable on good days in fine weather, but would lose money on inclement days. Its Thames career was pitifully short and *La Marguerite* was later transferred to serve in North Wales. It was joined by two other palatial large steamers: *Koh-i-Noor* of 1892, and *Royal Sovereign* of 1893. By 1895 these three large steamers were all operated by New Palace Steamers Limited. Each capable of

Golden Eagle initially operated the London to Margate and Ramsgate service. During the First World War it carried 518,101 troops across the English Channel. At the outbreak of the Second World War it carried evacuees to the safety of the east coast.

Pleasure steamers needed a great number of people to keep them operating during their short but busy summer season. Here cleaners precariously clean the massive paddle box of the *Crested Eagle* in April 1934.

around 20 knots, for a time they provided serious competition for the GSNC. With the potential to offer luxurious, fast and comfortable crossings to the Continent as well as trips to the coast, they played a major part in Thames excursion work. But, after a career of around ten years, their uneconomic fuel consumption and sheer size meant that profits were negligible. Only the *Royal Sovereign* remained on the Thames service, continuing in this role until 1929. Meanwhile, the GSNC had placed the distinctive *Crested Eagle* in service.

By the late 1880s east-coast resorts such as Clacton, Walton-on-the-Naze and Felixstowe were eager to seize a share of the enormous tripper market offered by London. By 1887 a steamer named *Clacton* was operating between London's Old Swan Pier and the growing Essex resort whose name it bore. It offered a round trip in a day, which would have been impossible in earlier years. As often happens, such a noble venture coincided with similar ambitions from other operators.

Unfortunately for them, the Clacton entrepreneurs' investment coincided with the building of the great 'Birds' of the GSNC fleet, and their enterprise failed. But, between 1890 and 1896, investors on the east coast purchased four splendid new steamers, built by the famed Denny of Dumbarton yard, for Thames and east-coast excursion service. *Clacton Belle*, *Woolwich Belle*, *London Belle* and *Southend Belle*, named after their calling points, became an efficient and versatile fleet. Such a splendid venture had to meet with some success and in 1897 the well-loved 'Belle Steamers' company was formed.

To reinforce the new branding, two new steamers were ordered, the *Walton Belle* and the *Yarmouth Belle*. After another change of company name, a final steamer, the *Southwold Belle* of 1900, completed the fleet. The owning company was canny in that it owned the piers as well as a grand hotel. It was to a great extent self-sufficient. In the first decade of the twentieth century confidence was at an all-time high and the Thames fleet was perhaps at its most magnificent, but inevitably, after a pinnacle is reached, there comes a fall. By 1911 the *Southwold Belle* was sold; the *Clacton Belle* followed soon after.

Away from the Thames, brothers Peter and Alec Campbell were well known for operating steamers on the Clyde, where their initial success with *Waverley* and *Bonnie Doon* persuaded them to relocate their business in the late 1880s to the Bristol Channel. Their company, P. & A. Campbell, was duly created.

Handbill for a Belle Steamer cruise to Clacton. With the demise of the company, the steamers were withdrawn and sold, but most found alternative roles in other areas of Britain.

Southend Belle was one of the famous Belle Steamers and was initially used on the route to Margate. The fleet was affected by charabancs and operated on longer, less profitable routes. The GSNC survived because it also operated many shorter Kent and Essex coast cruises.

Yarmouth Belle was built for the London to Great Yarmouth route and operated at a speed of 17 knots. It was sold to the New Medway Steam Packet Company in 1928 and was renamed *Queen of Southend*.

An officer aboard P. & A. Campbell's *Cambria* at Ilfracombe around 1904. Conditions could often be uncomfortable for officers as bridges on early paddle steamers were open to the elements, affording no shelter in wet and stormy conditions.

The first P. & A. Campbell paddle steamer was the *Ravenswood* of 1891. Soon after, *Westward Ho*, *Britannia* and *Cambria* were placed in service. Their most distinctive feature was a long and impressive promenade deck that ran the whole length of the steamer. These vessels provided the company with a splendid fleet to use during the great Edwardian heyday of pleasure steamers. The white-funnelled fleet was further enhanced by the acquisition of *Lady Ismay*, *Glen Avon* and *Glen Usk* in the years running up to the outbreak of the First World War. This proud fleet was superbly fit for purpose. The larger steamers were able to undertake excursion work at the height of the season, while the smaller ones enabled economical operation when trade was leaner at the start and end of the season.

An important aspect of the Bristol Channel service was the link between Weston-super-Mare and Penarth or Cardiff, which profitably catered for businessmen as well as holidaymakers. The short hop across the Bristol Channel was preferable to the roundabout route necessary by train or road. Peter and Alec Campbell did encounter some competition, one short-lived rival being the *Lady Gwendoline* of 1889. Perhaps the biggest threat came from the steamers of the Barry Railway, which entered the scene in 1905 with the *Devonia* and *Gwalia*. Contending that the operation of steamers by a railway company was illegal, and that it should stick to running trains, P. & A. Campbell challenged this competition in court. As a result, the Barry Railway was forced to limit the ports that its steamers could call at, thereby making its endeavour far from

The crew of the *Britannia* at Ilfracombe in October 1907. Many people were employed in the catering department on these steamers. This was also the time when paddle steamers were coal-fired and many men were needed as stokers.

Paddle steamers were always popular on the Bristol Channel. They were able easily to link towns on the Welsh and English coasts – journey time by road or rail would have taken a great deal longer.

profitable. By May 1910 the *Gwalia* was sold to the Furness Railway and, while the other steamers were used by a new company, they were eventually taken over by the mighty P. & A. Campbell towards the start of the First World War.

The Campbell fleet now looked unassailable – like the British Empire did at the time – but the steamers saw service in the First World War and, when it ended in 1918, some vessels had been lost and others required far too much work to make them suitable for service again. P. & A. Campbell withdrew these, and the company would struggle to return to its pre-war peak.

In North Wales, tugs and small companies battled over the pleasure-steamer business and it was not until 1891 that a dominant operator emerged – the Liverpool & North Wales Steamship Company. Further amalgamations followed in 1899 when the Snowdon Passenger Steamship Company was acquired. A consequence of such amalgamations was often that larger paddle steamers of the predominant company operated on the principal route, with smaller steamers sailing on feeder services and 'trips around the bay' from the main calling points. North Wales was an excellent example of this system, as large steamers such as *La Marguerite* would convey passengers from Liverpool to the principal North Wales pier at Llandudno, from where smaller but delightful steamers such as the *Snowdon* would take passengers on to the scenic beauties of the Menai Strait.

By the time of Queen Victoria's Diamond Jubilee in 1897, the paddle steamers of the south coast had perhaps reached their zenith. They were more plentiful, larger and more luxurious than they had ever been or would ever be.

The crowning moment was the impressive Fleet Review of 1897, when the Queen reviewed the Royal Navy in the Spithead at Portsmouth. The United Kingdom would never see such a spectacle again. The Spithead Review showed the features and potential of the south coast to visiting paddle steamers from areas such as the River Thames and the Bristol Channel. A result of this was that P. & A. Campbell entered the south-coast and Southampton market with the magnificent steamers *Cambria* and *Glen Rosa*.

Somewhat complacent after their long dominance of services in the area, Red Funnel placed the *Lorna Doone* in service in 1898, followed in 1900 by the *Balmoral*, operating in direct opposition to P. & A. Campbell's *Cambria*. Cosens, too, were determined to maintain their challenge and introduced *Majestic* in 1901 – just four months after the death of Queen Victoria.

Although Brighton had developed as a resort at the time of the Prince Regent, its heyday was at the very end of the nineteenth century, when the Palace Pier and West Pier were converted into vast hubs of exuberant seaside pleasure, along with extensive facilities for landing paddle steamers. The other main Sussex resorts, Eastbourne and Hastings, also developed paddle-steamer services among a welter of amalgamations and reorganisation in the last two decades of the nineteenth century. Nevertheless, the huge potential of the Sussex

North Wales was a wonderful location for pleasure steamers. Liverpool and Llandudno provided plenty of passengers for scenic cruises through the Menai Strait. Llandudno Pier also welcomed steamers to and from Blackpool and Southport.

Ticket for the Royal Naval Review of 26 June 1897 to mark the Diamond Jubilee of Queen Victoria. This historic event showed operators such as P. & A. Campbell the huge potential market offered by the south coast.

P. & A. CAMPBELL, Ltd.

Royal Naval Review, Spithead.

Her Majesty's Diamond Jubilee.
→ 1897. →

The *Worthing Belle* leaving Brighton. Paddle steamers used the Palace and West piers at Brighton. Cruises were offered to France, the Isle of Wight, Southampton, Deal and Dover.

market had been only modestly exploited, and the now mighty P. & A. Campbell, coveting a larger share of the huge south-coast business, extended their services along the coast to the major resorts of Brighton, Hastings and Eastbourne. Their steamers usually connected with others at Southampton and Portsmouth, and also with vessels sailing even further up the Channel into Kent.

Campbells took over steamers of the Brighton, Worthing & South Coast Steamboat Company in 1902 and set about transforming the fleet for their needs. The Sussex coast, with its extensive and exploited resorts, gave them the perfect operating area. Fine piers and landing facilities had been built, and the geographical position of the resorts meant that the company could run services to and from areas such as the Isle of Wight, Southampton, Bournemouth, Southsea, Deal and Folkestone, as well as trips across the Channel to Boulogne and Cherbourg. The densely printed handbills of the period show the sheer ambition of the company as well as the potential of the area. At the time, *Brighton Queen*, *Bonnie Doon*

and *Glen Rosa* undertook the cruises. The most exciting and longest cruises of all were when the steamers sailed from their home ports on the Bristol Channel to the Sussex coast at the start of each season, and then back again at the end.

Southampton services were invigorated by the arrival of new steamers in the Edwardian period, one of the earliest being the *Princess Royal* of 1906. In the summer of 1908 one of Bournemouth's best-loved steamers, *Bournemouth Queen*, entered service, and in the same year Cosens placed the *Emperor of India* in service.

Captain West, the master of the *Brighton Queen*, photographed in 1910, when P. & A. Campbell were expanding their services along the south coast.

The *Brighton Queen* departing from Ryde Pier on the Isle of Wight in August 1910. This was the heyday of paddle steamers in the United Kingdom and most seaside resorts were connected by an extensive network of steamer routes.

The Edwardian era on the south coast was therefore a period of change. Some companies disappeared while others merged to provide a leaner and

The *Emperor of India*, having just departed from Bournemouth Pier. This vessel was built by Thornycroft in 1906 and after lengthening was sold to Cosens. It was withdrawn in 1956.

less competitive arena of operation. This resulted in several steamers being withdrawn, among them the *Brodick Castle*. In a final flurry of activity before the First World War, Cosens introduced the steamers *Melcombe Regis* and *Alexandra*. These new additions were welcome but they were not revolutionary. The new arrivals could have been described as 'charming' rather than 'impressive'.

Albert Victor departing from Weymouth. Cosens were closely associated with Weymouth, operating many famous steamers such as *Emperor of India*, *Empress*, *Monarch*, *Premier* and *Consul* along the Dorset coastline until the 1960s.

25

QUEEN LINE OF
PLEASURE STEAMERS

(NEW MEDWAY STEAM PACKET COMPANY LIMITED

3D

BETWEEN THE WARS

THE END OF THE Edwardian era and the First World War brought massive changes to everyday life in the United Kingdom. Obviously, pleasure steamers would suffer as well. When the war commenced, the British Empire was at its height, and on the south coast a very impressive twenty-four paddle steamers were plying for trade. Inevitably, several of these well-loved pleasure steamers were lost or sunk during the war.

The First World War resulted in many technological advances as well as changes in people's attitudes and ways of life. Motor vehicles were gaining in popularity, and with them came the widespread introduction of the charabanc or large open motor coach, which for the first time allowed working-class people to travel together in relative comfort to the coast by road. As a means of transport, it was both more flexible and less weather-reliant than the paddle steamer.

Motor cars were also becoming the ultimate aspiration of the middle classes and, as they became more popular, so they became more affordable. It was only a matter of time before the charabanc and the motor car would present a serious threat to the pleasure steamer. Operators were of course aware of this and reacted by introducing new pleasure steamers. These ships were mostly turbine steamers or motor vessels. This new tonnage was sleek, luxurious and fast, reflecting the age in which it was built. This was the era of the ocean liner, and graceful, stylish travel was the mark of the age. Steamship operators sought to transfer this ambience to their humble pleasure vessels.

Some operators were unable to transform their vision into reality and the service they provided did not always coincide with what passengers wanted from a day at the coast. Transport was changing, but people were changing as well. They were becoming more ambitious in their needs both for a day out and in their home life. Mass entertainment and consumerism were taking hold for the first time and this affected pleasure-steamer services. The growth of the radio, cinema and variety theatre and an interest in hobbies and outdoor activities meant that a week at the seaside was no

Opposite:
Cover for the New Medway Steam Packet Company's 1934 brochure. It advertised their services on the River Medway and Thames estuary, as well as providing a guide to places visited by the steamers.

longer the only aim of holidaymakers. Now, the prospect of a camping or touring holiday was becoming a reality.

Operators therefore saw the 1920s and 1930s as a time to change services and to create a timetable that was leaner and more reflective of the age and its needs. Tradition had little relevance to this world, and uneconomic routes were withdrawn or replaced. Fewer pleasure steamers were being

P. & A. Campbell became the key operator on the Bristol Channel. This brochure dates from the 1930s and advertises their cruises to resorts such as Ilfracombe, Weston-super-Mare and Minehead.

The observation lounge of the *Royal Eagle*. Pleasure steamers usually had different areas for different classes of passenger. Passengers would have to pay a small fee to use facilities such as this.

The *Compton Castle* at Dartmouth around 1958. Despite being small, it could carry over five hundred passengers. Steamers such as *Compton Castle* were built specifically to work on the River Dart. Steamers like these often linked small communities with markets and nearby villages, as well as providing a tourist-based service.

built, although this was not always evident as many Victorian paddle steamers were still in service, while the excitement of the new, larger motor ships disguised the fact that services were contracting.

The Liverpool & North Wales Steamship Company was one of the first to turn away from paddle propulsion and to place in service a twin-screw turbine steamer. Introduced in 1914, the *St Seiriol* was lost during the First World War, but it had marked the way forward. The large and majestic *La Marguerite* was withdrawn in 1925. The North Wales company naturally chose a turbine steamer to replace it, the *St Tudno*, entering service in 1926. Although looking very different to *La Marguerite*, the *St Tudno* could carry 2,493 passengers at a speed of up to 19 knots in luxury. Within five years, it was joined by a new *St Seiriol*. Although smaller, it could convey passengers at around the same speed and proved to be versatile. In 1936 the splendid

La Marguerite became a great favourite in North Wales. It was a massive 330 feet in length and had a trial speed of 21 knots. It had large bunkers capable of holding 100 tons of coal. Before the First World War it had a crew of ninety-five.

little *St Silio* entered service on the North Wales run, confirming the confidence in the future of pleasure steamers in that area. The decade was characterised by the withdrawal of elderly paddle steamers and their replacement by turbine steamers, which were not only new, but also more economic and more versatile.

During the 1920s the River Medway fleet of the New Medway Steam Packet Company expanded rapidly. The Medway Steam Packet Company had been long established, but its new incarnation as the New Medway Steam Packet Company was to cause a revolution. The original pre-war company had in its fleet several aged paddle steamers. The best-known of these were the *Princess of Wales* and the *City of Rochester*. These traditional steamers operated from a base at Chatham on the Medway and, after service during the First World War, returned to operation in 1920.

The new company had an ambitious and talented new director, Captain Sidney Shippick, who had operated a couple of small paddle steamers on the south coast. One of these was the delightful little *Audrey* and he immediately set about operating it for his new company. From the modest beginnings of the Strood to Southend service, the company soon ventured further afield to places as far away as Great Yarmouth and across the English Channel to Boulogne and Calais. The year 1924 was a defining one for the company for it was then that the *Medway Queen* entered service on the Medway and Thames. Built by Ailsa of Troon, the *Medway Queen* was to become one of the fondest-remembered steamers of the NMSPC fleet, and its story is still unfolding today.

Shippick's ambitions required the rapid expansion of the fleet in order to operate the new routes. Two early additions were ex-Admiralty minesweepers from the First World War. These distinctive two-funnelled paddle steamers, renamed *Queen of Kent* and *Queen of Thanet*, operated services that included the Continent and up the east coast as far as Great Yarmouth. The NMSPC also acquired the *Yarmouth Belle* and renamed it *Queen of Southend*.

The River Medway was transformed during the 1920s when Captain Shippick managed the New Medway Steam Packet Company. The older steamers were gradually replaced by a revolutionary fleet of sleek motor ships of 'The Queen Line'.

A unique feature of paddle steamers was the paddle boxes. These often incorporated carved wooden designs showing places of interest, historical figures or flags linked with the steamer's name. This is the paddle box of the *Medway Queen* at Strood in 1962.

Royal Eagle was the last paddle steamer to be built by the General Steam Navigation Company and entered service in 1932. After the Second World War it proved to be too large for economic service and was withdrawn in 1949.

Handbill for cruises on the River Medway in Kent during July 1936. 'The Queen Line', under the management of Captain Shippick, used publicity to good effect. The steamers had a wide variety of facilities over several decks.

Paddle-steamer operation had little scope for nostalgia and Shippick soon despatched the gallant little *Audrey* to the scrapyard. By the end of the 1920s Sidney Shippick's New Medway Steam Packet Company fleet became known as 'The Queen Line', a name that summed up his lofty ambitions for the company. Its advertising material of the time shows that Shippick had a great flair for publicising his steamers. His style was bold and left potential passengers in no doubt that they ought to travel by 'The Queen Line'.

One area where pleasure steamers seemed to be succeeding was the River Thames. The Wall Street Crash of 1929 and the Great Depression that followed affected steamer services. The GSNC and NMSPC fleets survived more or less unscathed. The most spectacular arrival on the Thames during this period was the splendid *Royal Eagle* of 1932. Built for the General

Steam Navigation Company fleet by Cammell Laird on the River Mersey, *Royal Eagle* provided spectacularly fitted-out interiors, the most striking feature of which was the vast observation lounge. Her master at the time was the jovial Captain Bill Branthwaite.

Just a few years later, in 1935, London gained its most revolutionary new arrival in the form of the *Queen of the Channel*. The first twin-screw motor vessel to serve on the Thames, it was built by the famed Denny of Dumbarton yard and was a glorious addition to the GSNC fleet. With large and comfortable saloons (some of which were oddly decorated in a mock-Tudor half-timbered style), she soon embarked on rapid and efficient services from London to the Continent, visiting Boulogne, Calais and Ostend, cruising at an impressive speed of 19 knots.

These stylish new motor ships reinvigorated services on the Thames and Medway. Passengers adored the *Queen of the Channel* and within two years another new vessel was built for the Thames service. The *Royal Sovereign* could whisk passengers from London to the Continent at a speed of 21 knots. Also in that year, the two main companies in the Thames service combined

Captain William Branthwaite of 'Eagle Steamers' watching men being prepared to entertain passengers in 1935. Steamer companies often provided entertainment for their passengers. This included singers, competitions and characters roaming the decks.

when the General Steam Navigation Company bought shares in the New Medway Steam Packet Company, though both companies generally kept their separate identities. Towards the end of the 1930s the *Queen of Kent* and *Queen of Thanet* were laid up owing to their high running costs. The *Isle of Arran* had been withdrawn a couple of years earlier.

In the summer of 1939 the *Royal Daffodil* entered service, with its role on the London river seemingly assured. Built by Denny of Dumbarton, and the epitome of elegance and good design, the *Royal Daffodil* was perhaps the best-loved of all Thames pleasure steamers. Its arrival almost coincided with the Holidays with Pay Act of 1938. Pleasure-steamer operators may have seen this as the perfect opportunity to attract an even bigger clientele for a day or holiday by the sea, but this did not happen, because people now had a greater range of activities to choose from. There was a modest rise in passenger numbers, but it was not what had been hoped for.

South-coast services were reinvigorated by the addition of new but similar tonnage during the 1920s. One of the best-known was the *Princess Elizabeth* of 1927, named after the young princess who would one day become Queen. The *Gracie Fields* was the last paddle steamer to be built for the Southampton service as motor vessels were to become the norm in the years after. Cosens, though, still preferred paddle power and in 1937 they acquired the *Duke of Devonshire* and renamed it *Consul*. It was soon joined by the *Embassy*.

By the outbreak of the Second World War, the pleasure-steamer scene in the United Kingdom had seen two decades of slow decline. It was a time when change was visible. The splendid *Royal Daffodil* of the General Steam Navigation Company fleet was the embodiment of this new age – a large, sleek and modern steamer capable of providing a fast and relatively economic service. It was the 'poor man's liner' but did it represent a future that could be sustained?

Holidays in Belgium

THE
New ROUTE TO

OSTEND

DIRECT FROM THE HEART OF LONDON
by the new motor vessels

ROYAL SOVEREIGN

OR

QUEEN OF THE CHANNEL

leaving
TOWER OF LONDON PIER 8.40 a.m.
(Adjoining Mark Lane Stn. Underground)
arriving OSTEND about 3 p.m.
every SATURDAY and SUNDAY
From 25th June to
Mid-September 1938.
Calling at SOUTHEND.

FIRST CLASS ACCOMMODATION
AT TOURIST RATES

The new motor vessels *Royal Sovereign* and *Queen of the Channel* offered 1930s passengers fast weekend services to Ostend from London. Both ships were lost during the Second World War but were later replaced.

Opposite: Embarking passengers on the *Crested Eagle* at Tower Pier, London, in August 1935. Pleasure steamer cruises from London were hugely popular. Embarking and disembarking passengers needed to be carried out quickly and efficiently at each pier.

35

Royal Daffodil
at Tower Pier,
London, on the
day of its maiden
voyage, 27 May
1939. *Royal
Daffodil* was the
epitome of sleek
1930s design on
the River Thames
and showed how
pleasure-steamer
design had
developed.

The Second World War interrupted the careers of every pleasure steamer in Britain. Within hours of Britain's entry into the war, many steamers were requisitioned by the government to take evacuee children to the safety of towns far away from the cities targeted by the Luftwaffe. After this duty, steamers adopted a wartime grey camouflage livery instead of the bright colours of their peacetime role – which many steamers would never resume. Although not evident at the time, the role of the pleasure steamer would never return to its pre-war eminence.

Ryde was requisitioned at the outbreak of the Second World War. It became a paddle minesweeper and is shown here in its wartime camouflage.

DECLINE OF THE PADDLE STEAMERS

T HE Second World War changed a great deal, and pleasure steamers did not adapt after they returned battered by the ravages of war. Instead, operators eagerly accepted the compensation for wartime losses offered by the government, and they quickly set about rebuilding damaged vessels or replacing lost ships with almost identical new tonnage. Initially, this seemed to be a good move. Demobbed servicemen quickly returned to life in 'Civvy Street' and were eager to resume the carefree life of pre-war years, part of which was the happy and nostalgic family outing to the seaside by pleasure steamer.

The mid- to late 1940s were an Indian summer for Britain's pleasure steamers. Typical of the initial post-war confidence was the Bristol Channel operator P. & A. Campbell. The company suffered major losses during the Second World War and its post-1946 fleet had been depleted by five steamers. Two splendid new paddle steamers were ordered by P. & A. Campbell to help compensate for their wartime casualties. They were the *Bristol Queen* of 1946 and the *Cardiff Queen* of 1947.

Campbells ended the 1940s with the largest fleet of any pleasure-steamer operator, having seven large steamers at their disposal. Despite having this significant fleet, they suffered the problems that beset the other operators around the United Kingdom in that most of their steamers were becoming old and needed attention. They had also been through a vigorous wartime career. Tastes were also changing and many passengers wanted a sleek new steamer, whether it was a motor ship or a paddle steamer. *Cardiff Queen* and *Bristol Queen* were splendid new ships, but their lives would be limited because of their size and uneconomic operation. The burden of running the older, more cash-hungry steamers would eventually bring things to a swift close.

The position was similar on the Thames. When the Second World War ended just six steamers were left for River Thames service. These were quickly reconditioned and in 1946 the *Royal Eagle* and *Queen of Thanet* re-entered service. In 1948 the new *Queen of the Channel* and *Royal Sovereign* entered service to replace the steamers of the same names lost during the conflict.

Opposite:
Cardiff Queen at Cardiff on 29 May 1964. The well-loved *Cardiff Queen* and *Bristol Queen* had very short careers as part of the P. & A. Campbell fleet. They survived for just a little over twenty years before being scrapped.

Monarch on the Cosens slipway at Weymouth in 1946. This image shows numbering on the hull where plates were replaced. Many steamers were lost in the Second World War and many others required major rebuilding afterwards.

In 1949 Red Funnel ordered the motor ship *Balmoral*, which would become one of their most famous and long-lived vessels. *Balmoral* was built as a ferry crossing between Southampton and Cowes but also carried out extensive excursion cruise work. Its design, facilities and seaworthiness were exemplary. The former *Queen of Kent* and *Queen of Thanet* were also acquired and renamed by the company but proved surplus to requirements as the post-war decline in passenger traffic had started.

Other pleasure steamers on the south coast were sold or withdrawn. This meant that post-war fleets were leaner and more reflective of new conditions. Inevitably, by the mid-1950s, the post-war shrinkage of fleets was becoming more acute. Old favourites such as the *Emperor of India* and *Bournemouth Queen* were withdrawn in 1957. The Cosens and Red Funnel fleets became a pale reflection of their former selves. Red Funnel was fortunate in having other options for the future with the introduction of car ferries. Red Funnel therefore started to switch from carrying passengers to cars and by 1965 *Balmoral* became the last Red Funnel excursion steamer.

On the Clyde and Loch Lomond the traditional paddle steamer was still the preferred type of vessel. Two of the most famous of all paddle steamers were to emerge from the famous Glasgow yard of A. & J. Inglis in those post-war years – *Waverley* and *Maid of the Loch*.

Bristol Queen under construction at the Charles Hill yard in 1945–6. Ample government grants for war losses allowed several new and very large pleasure steamers to be built at the end of the war.

Waverley was built for the London & North Eastern Railway (LNER) for service on the Firth of Clyde and was a replacement for a steamer of the same name lost at Dunkirk. The last paddle steamer to be built for Firth of Clyde services, *Waverley* was launched on 2 October 1946, entering service on 16 June 1947. It cruised on the route for which it had been built – up Loch Goil and Loch Long to Arrochar and Lochgoilhead, part of the famed 'Three Lochs Tour' linking in with a cruise on Loch Lomond.

Passengers enjoying their trip to the seaside aboard the *Royal Eagle* in 1946. Pleasure steamers could carry over two thousand passengers. In good weather, the best place to be was on deck enjoying the company of family and friends.

Maid of the Loch
on Loch Lomond.
Although most
paddle steamers
operated in rivers
and estuaries,
some sailed on
lakes and inland
lochs such as
Loch Lomond,
where *Maid of
the Loch* could
be seen from
1953 onwards.

Waverley later saw service on the ferry routes from Wemyss Bay and Gourock. Its itinerary was periodically modified as piers closed and passenger traffic altered. Its livery likewise changed to reflect several changes in ownership. Despite the Firth of Clyde retaining a strong cruising tradition, steamers were gradually withdrawn. These included the splendid *Jeanie Deans* in 1961, *Talisman* in 1966 and *Caledonia* in 1969. *Waverley* then remained as the Firth of Clyde's last paddle steamer.

The *Maid of the Loch* was the final large paddle steamer to be built in the United Kingdom and entered service on Loch Lomond in 1953. *Maid of the Loch* was taken in sections from the Inglis yard, where it was built, by rail to Balloch to be reassembled. With a service speed of 12 knots, *Maid of the Loch* proved to be a first-class steamer from the viewpoint of passengers, but by the start of the 1960s losses on the Loch Lomond service were becoming apparent, and the 1960s and 1970s were characterised by threats of closure and uncertainty. By 1981 Caledonian MacBrayne reported huge losses and *Maid of the Loch* was withdrawn from service.

People's lifestyles were changing faster than ever before, influenced by new forms of transport, developing technology and the growth of consumerism. Steamer operators had reacted in the past by thinning down fleets, cutting out uneconomic routes and building bigger and more efficient steamers. Now, the media and advertising were making people aware that

A P. & A. Campbell steamer in the process of being scrapped at Newport on 29 October 1955. By this time, the post-war boom was over and many paddle steamers were being scrapped.

The dining saloon of the *Maid of the Loch*. Passengers could combine a meal in good surroundings while admiring the glorious scenery through large windows. *Maid of the Loch* remained in service on Loch Lomond until 1981.

they had a choice of where they spent their holiday, and it was not just a choice of whether to go to Southend or to Margate, but rather whether to go to the seaside, or to go camping, or, for the better-off and more adventurous, to take a continental holiday.

The decline of the British pleasure steamer was rapid during the 1950s. Every year brought news of another favourite steamer being withdrawn from service and eventually scrapped.

Tower Bridge
and the Tower
of London were
favourite places
to photograph a
pleasure steamer.
By the early 1950s
Royal Eagle and
Golden Eagle
had both
been scrapped.
Crested Eagle
had been lost
during the war.

During the 1950s
and early 1960s
Cosens of
Weymouth
operated the
well-loved *Consul*
(shown here),
Embassy and
Monarch along the
south coast. By
1966 all three had
been withdrawn
from service.

The River Thames was no exception to the rule. The fine *Golden Eagle* did not enter service until 1950, but, soon after, the famed *Royal Eagle* was scrapped. The withdrawals levelled out towards the end of the decade, by which time most of the older and more expensive to operate paddle steamers had gone. The three motor ships were almost new and were therefore safe in the short term, but their size was uneconomic for their post-war role. Timetable tweaks were made and a new pier at Deal made a welcome addition to the calling points in 1957. This to a small extent increased confidence.

By the 1960s the GSNC was introducing gimmicks to entice passengers, but the arrival of bingo, one-armed bandits and 'rock and roll' cruises did little to help. The Thames, though, still had the three mighty motor ships *Royal Daffodil*, *Royal Sovereign* and *Queen of the Channel*. At around 300 feet in length and with passenger accommodation for up to 2,385, vessels such as the *Royal Daffodil* could never have a financially secure future. When it departed for the scrapyard, regular passengers realised that the unthinkable had happened.

After the Second World War, Cosens resumed services on much the same lines as before. They were lucky as they had suffered no losses. Withdrawals were made, but the post-war years were characterised by the running of the three venerable paddle steamers *Consul*, *Embassy* and *Monarch*. After post-war refits, all three steamers happily plied for Weymouth trade through the 1950s despite the inevitable decline of services nationally. *Monarch* was withdrawn in 1961; the delightful *Consul* followed in 1962 and, just four years later, the final one, *Embassy*, was withdrawn.

Sussex coast services by P. & A. Campbell became an early casualty of the decline. By 1950 services were undertaken by the *Glen Gower* alone. The splendid new *Cardiff Queen* made an appearance on the Sussex station in 1952 and 1953 before the *Glen Gower* returned to Brighton in 1956. Within a year, P. & A. Campbell withdrew their service on the south coast. The position had certainly changed since the heady days of the Fleet Review for Queen Victoria's Diamond Jubilee some sixty years earlier.

Meanwhile on the Bristol Channel, economic problems forced P. & A. Campbell to withdraw *Ravenswood* and *Britannia* in the 1950s. By the end of that decade P. & A. Campbell were in serious financial trouble and became part of another company. Although services did continue into the 1960s, further steamers were withdrawn, one at a time. The company also ventured into North Wales cruising with

Brochure advertising day trips to France by the White Funnel fleet in 1955. Pleasure steamers provided the only opportunity of visiting France for most people. The steamer crossing took around four hours from Eastbourne to Boulogne.

the purchase of the *St Trillo*. It was operated both in North Wales and on the Bristol Channel, along with the *Westward Ho*.

Towards the end of the 1960s, P. & A. Campbell chartered the former Isles of Scilly steamer *Queen of the Isles* and the former Red Funnel ship *Balmoral* for further service on their routes. The more economic motor ships spelled the end for the two large paddle steamers that remained. Soon after, the majestic *Cardiff Queen* and *Bristol Queen* were scrapped. This was just twenty years after they had entered service.

In North Wales, once the wartime grey paint had been removed, the three steamers re-entered service very much to the timetable of pre-war days. But by the late 1950s there was a serious drop in passenger traffic and within a few years the *St Tudno* and *St Seiriol* had been withdrawn. The gallant little *St Trillo* struggled on for a few more years until it too was scrapped. P. & A. Campbell bravely fought to keep the service alive, but enthusiasm, nostalgia and a little bit of madness were not enough to sustain profitability. If the public's tastes have changed and they want something different, then no amount of brave new initiatives can help.

Brochure advertising cruises on the Firth of Clyde and Loch Lomond by the Caledonian Steam Packet Company in 1963.

Princess Elizabeth at Weymouth pleasure pier in September 1964. *Princess Elizabeth* was then owned by Herbert Jennings, who endeavoured to operate it at places such as Weymouth, Lyme Regis and Torquay. The venture eventually failed.

The last bastion of the paddle steamers, the Firth of Clyde had by the 1950s seen some modernisation. The Clyde differed from the rest of Britain in that the geography of western Scotland meant that the total replacement of the steamer by cars would never be possible. Services did adapt, with a rise in the number of car ferries, so that passengers could take their cars with them by ferry to explore a holiday island by road instead of by foot. The traditional 'doon the watter' trade from Glasgow did remain popular. Bute, Arran and Cowal were by now the most popular destinations. One by one, the old paddle steamers were withdrawn, to be replaced by less characterful ferries.

In 1959 a major preservation group had been formed because it seemed that the pleasure steamer was facing extinction. Within little more than a decade, that was indeed the case. The holiday industry and leisure market developed beyond recognition in the 1960s. An old paddle steamer was far less attractive to most people than a modern plane or car. In common with the steamers that had once disgorged countless thousands of happy holidaymakers, seaside resorts now faced the same fate. It was the end of the traditional British seaside holiday and, although the seaside remained popular for several more decades, the resorts never seemed to have that same sparkle and attraction that they had in the past.

Queen Mary II became a great survivor on the Firth of Clyde. Turbine steamers, as well as paddle steamers, remained popular on the Clyde until the 1970s.

PRESERVATION
AND OPERATION

The popular Firth of Clyde paddle steamer *Caledonia* alongside Campbeltown in 1964. Despite the protestations of enthusiasts, *Caledonia* was withdrawn in 1969 and later ended up on the Thames Embankment in London as a floating restaurant and bar.

W HO would have thought in those ultra-modern years of the 1960s that what we now call 'heritage' would one day become trendy and popular again? With the formation of the Civic Trust in 1957, and with all things Victorian being eloquently championed by such as Sir John Betjeman, the fussy wood-panelled interiors, the attention to detail and the style of the past became a marketable product. It soon became evident that people felt nostalgic about the past and, although they wanted to live in modern homes, they liked to spend some of their increasing leisure time in the nostalgic world of the past.

The early 1960s were the final years of the *Medway Queen*, which by 1963 was becoming old and required a major survey and work to enable it to continue in service. Money was not plentiful in those declining years. The loss

Medway Queen departing from Southend Pier in July 1963. Just two months later it was withdrawn from service.

of the vessel's calling points at Chatham Sun Pier and Sheerness reduced its passenger base. Despite a new calling point being made available at Strood, passengers were becoming less willing to put themselves out; the convenience of the motor car had generated a new attitude.

The withdrawal of the Dunkirk veteran *Medway Queen* in September 1963 focused awareness on the plight of the paddle steamer. The interest of that great defender of our heritage Sir John Betjeman drew attention to its plight. Preservationists strove hard to ensure that the *Medway Queen* was saved, but, more than once, it looked as though the battle was lost as the *Medway Queen* faced a less than dignified end. Static preservation in connection with the Forte catering empire looked to be the most likely fate of the *Medway Queen* but, when this failed, it eventually found a role as a clubhouse for a marina on the River Medina on the Isle of Wight. Initially the venture was a success as the vessel lay alongside the later withdrawn *Ryde* from the Portsmouth to Ryde route. But, as debts rose and costs increased, the *Medway Queen* again faced a period of uncertainty. This was made worse by questions over its ownership. The 1970s were to become the 'graveyard years' of the pleasure steamers, and the *Medway Queen* fell further into decline.

The south coast did, however, see a rare expansion of services in the early 1960s. The *Freshwater* was acquired in 1959 by Herbert Jennings, who renamed it *Sussex Queen* and operated it for a couple of years, but, inevitably, in the prevailing atmosphere of the time, it was later withdrawn. The *Freshwater* was the stimulus for the formation of the Paddle Steamer Preservation Society in 1959 when the decline and plight of the paddle steamer was noted.

The *Freshwater* operating from Lymington in the late 1950s. The withdrawal of this paddle steamer resulted in the formation of a major paddle-steamer preservation group in 1959.

Princess Elizabeth was also acquired for further service at Bournemouth, Weymouth and Torquay from 1962 onwards. This also failed. The fine little *Consul* was operated along the Sussex coast at places such as Brighton, Eastbourne and Hastings, as well as on the River Thames, in 1963. This too was a failure and *Consul* was placed for further service at Weymouth in 1964. Yet again the result was failure and, in 1966, the *Embassy* was withdrawn. South coast paddle-steamer services had ceased.

Handbill for a special charter sailing of the *Princess Elizabeth* to Torquay in June 1965. At the time, special cruises were organised to promote the heritage of pleasure steamers, to increase passenger numbers and to assist operators.

In 1966 an ambitious project took shape when the *Jeanie Deans* arrived on the Thames from the Firth of Clyde. The perhaps foolhardy conversion of this steamer into the *Queen of the South* was an exciting move for enthusiasts, but technical problems plagued the vessel from the start and cruises were soon abandoned. The resulting

Embassy at Bournemouth. During the late 1950s and early 1960s pleasure-steamer fleets shrank dramatically as the car gained popularity. Operators such as Cosens of Weymouth managed to survive until the mid-1960s but were eventually defeated by changing tastes.

unreliable service and bad publicity meant that a great deal of confidence was lost. *Queen of the South* survived for another season but by 1967 it had followed the rest to the breaker's yard.

All areas, apart from the Firth of Clyde, were now in the same position, but a key player in the future of paddle steamers was quietly going about its daily routine of cruising on the Firth. It would be over a decade before things would change dramatically for the rest of Britain with the arrival of the paddle steamer *Waverley*. The future belonged to *Waverley*.

The *Consul* at Southend Pier in September 1963. Its charter by New Belle Steamers was not a success on the Thames, but it did give valuable experience in operating a paddle steamer that was later used by Don Rose with the *Queen of the South*.

Queen of the South
at London in 1967.
The *Queen of*
the South had
a disappointing
and short career
on the Thames.
Many days were
lost to mechanical
failure. After debts
mounted, it
was withdrawn
in 1967.

The preservation movement had by the mid-1960s become largely a body that relied on memories and collecting old postcards rather than one that operated steamers. By the middle of the 1970s this had changed and the word 'preservation' needed to be replaced with the word 'operation'.

The preservationists soon realised that the best way to keep the memory alive might be to keep a steamer actually operational. The initial candidate was the Neyland ferry *Alumchine*. This fine little paddle steamer was small enough to be economic to run, and negotiations to purchase her commenced. Sadly, these came to nothing.

In 1965 the charming River Dart paddle steamer *Kingswear Castle* was offered to the preservationists for the modest sum of £600 as a gesture by the River Dart Steamboat Company, which felt sentimental about its last operational paddle steamer. The *Kingswear Castle* offered immense potential.

The steamer was acquired, but enthusiasts lacked the knowledge or impetus to restore and operate it. It was initially towed to the Isle of Wight to lie alongside the *Medway Queen*. Vandalism and lack of regular attention resulted in the need to decide whether to restore or dispose of the ship. Luckily, a positive decision was made and the *Kingswear Castle* was towed to the River Medway for restoration in 1971.

Kingswear Castle was withdrawn from service in 1965. Over the next few years it suffered a great deal of damage and decay before a full restoration took place. It is shown here in the late 1960s.

By the early 1970s, an active and well-organised group was attempting to raise awareness of the post-war paddle steamer *Waverley*, which had become the last of the line on the Firth of Clyde after the withdrawal of all its fleet mates. *Waverley* may have been neither the finest nor the favourite Clyde steamer of all time, but its importance came in being the last. Publicity was

In the mid-1960s the *Alumchine* was identified as the most suitable paddle steamer for preservation, owing to its size and condition. It was felt that the best way to preserve the heritage of the paddle steamer would be through maintaining a working example.

Waverley cruising on the Firth of Clyde before withdrawal from service in 1973. During the early 1970s *Waverley*'s uniqueness was promoted and special sailings and changes of livery were made to emphasise its special role.

focused on it, and changes of livery were used to promote its uniqueness. This was rewarded when it was surprisingly offered to the Paddle Steamer Preservation Society in November 1973 for the modest sum of £1.

This generous and somewhat unreal gesture was accepted. The challenges were immense and in those first few months *Waverley*'s future was debated as various options were explored for both a static and an operational role. The new owners bravely decided to operate the steamer, although it was the worst time in which to do so. Hard work, determination and a little bit of madness went into a major fundraising campaign. Against all odds, *Waverley* entered its preservation career in May 1975 amid a blaze of publicity. Its former striking LNER livery was restored to herald the new beginning.

By the late 1970s *Waverley* had shown a degree of success and the fact that it was still cruising showed that there was potential, albeit limited, in operating pleasure steamers. The acquisition and operation of *Waverley* was a huge boost to the *Kingswear Castle*. A small but dedicated band of volunteers now worked with a new impetus to restore it too. Funds were allocated to speed up the work and to finance specialist work that could not be done by the volunteers themselves.

Waverley's operation in England from 1978 onwards enabled a new public to be gained, and funds and fans built up. By November 1983, *Kingswear Castle* was steamed for the first time again. The bigger *Waverley* now belonged to the whole of the United Kingdom following its journeys around Britain's coastline. In 1984, when the *Waverley* and *Kingswear Castle* met on the River Medway for the first time, two dreams had become reality.

By the early 1980s nostalgia for the paddle steamer had been well and truly established with the success of the *Waverley* and *Kingswear Castle*. A further notable success was the restoration and reintroduction of the famous *Balmoral* as a companion for *Waverley* in 1986. *Balmoral* performed a vitally important role as it increased the number of piers served by the steamers as well as operating as a back-up if *Waverley* failed. *Balmoral* was also able to call at many long-forgotten places that were not accessible to *Waverley*.

This success, however, was balanced by the failure of other preservation projects. The *Caledonia*, *Lincoln Castle* and *Ryde* failed to establish any long-term

Kingswear Castle cruising in the River Thames in the mid-1980s. By this time, Waverley, Balmoral and Kingswear Castle were all providing cruises around the British coastline.

Balmoral approaching Southend Pier in 2009. It was originally built for service between Southampton and the Isle of Wight for Red Funnel Steamers. The windowed area at the stern was once a small car deck.

55

Paddle steamers operated on the River Humber up to the 1970s. *Tattershall Castle* found a long-lasting home as a static restaurant and bar on the Thames Embankment in London. *Wingfield Castle* and *Lincoln Castle* also found static roles. Attempts to restore the *Lincoln Castle* ended when it was scrapped in 2010.

Many paddle steamers became derelict and faced uncertain futures in the 1970s. Here, the *Medway Queen* is shown in poor condition, tied up against the former Royal Naval Dockyard at Chatham in the mid-1980s.

prospects. They were now operating in a very different world to that of their origin. New regulations, lack of funds, increased passenger expectations and the disappearance of seaside piers at which they could call combined to ensure that they would meet a negative end.

Other pleasure steamers such as the *Tattershall Castle*, *Princess Elizabeth* and *Wingfield Castle* found safety in a static role. By the mid-1980s the future was looking brighter for one steamer when a newly formed preservation group came to the rescue of the *Medway Queen*, which was later taken back to its

native River Medway. Further years of uncertainty followed and piecemeal work was undertaken to try to keep the steamer stable at its new temporary home at Damhead Creek.

By the start of the twenty-first century, it was left to *Waverley*, *Balmoral* and *Kingswear Castle* to carry on the operational tradition. By this time, pleasure steamers were entering a different world, where habits were changing again. The internet was revolutionising the way that people accessed information and spent their money. People were now able to find out everything about a pleasure steamer from their own personal computer. The handbills and long-established marketing methods of the past were gradually giving way to a new way of marketing services online.

By this time too the Heritage Lottery Fund had emerged as a major funder of steam preservation projects. The rebuilding of the *Waverley* in 2000 and its restoration to pristine 1947 condition was a remarkable example of the benefits of the Fund. This important work enabled expensive winter refit work to be cut.

Similarly, *Balmoral* and *Kingswear Castle* were awarded Heritage Lottery Fund cash. The Heritage Lottery Fund also awarded a grant to rebuild the *Medway Queen*'s hull. The steamer was gradually dismantled and transported to Bristol, where it gained a new and watertight hull, ensuring that it would have a future in the twenty-first century.

Another important preservation project was the *Maid of the Loch*, which throughout the 1990s and into the following century was gradually restored by a keen band of volunteers, in readiness for service again on Loch Lomond. By 2012, two hundred years after the birth of the *Comet*, the paddle steamer was still alive and showing a great deal of resilience.

Below left:
By the mid-1990s maintenance costs were escalating and new safety regulations threatened *Waverley*'s future. As a response, in 2000, *Waverley* was extensively rebuilt to its 1947 condition.

Overleaf:
Waverley approaching Clevedon Pier on the Bristol Channel in 2006, after its rebuilding. Note the brown deck houses. These aluminium structures were hand-grained to resemble wood panelling.

CONCLUSION

THE PLEASURE STEAMER was very much a product of Victorian and Edwardian times, when paddle propulsion was used extensively for transporting passengers to the seaside or overseas, as well as carrying goods to market.

There was always something attractive about a paddle steamer. Pleasure steamers were given appealing names that often reflected their geographic location, or commemorated an important figure, or provided a link to history. The often beautifully carved and decorated paddle boxes made a statement about the steamer and gave it a certain dignified charm and grace rarely found in any other form of transport. Its passenger accommodation often became grand, stylish and comfortable.

So, with just a handful of these beautiful old steamers still operating, what makes them so special? For some, it is their heritage. Many love to look back nostalgically at the well-remembered operating companies of yesteryear such as the Eagle Steamers and Cosens. For others, it is an 'experience' – a tourist attraction that needs to be sampled. But for most, pleasure steamers enable us to escape from everyday life and to enjoy the sensory pleasures of polished brass, fresh sea breezes, fluttering flags and the constantly changing elements.

Paddle steamers enjoyed their heyday in Victorian and Edwardian times. These steamers linked the many seaside resorts around the coast of Britain and enabled many people to enjoy a day at the seaside.

These delights, combined with the glories of the British coastline, make a cruise on a pleasure steamer very special. There is no better way to discover Britain's coast than on a pleasure steamer, and there is no nicer seaside view than that of a good-looking pleasure steamer tied up alongside a seaside pier.

Like the 1930s and 1950s before, the first decade or so of the twenty-first century brought a change in the fortunes of steamers and the needs of their passengers. It was also a time when new and exciting opportunities were there ready to be grasped. Pleasure steamers have always faced periods of great change. Boom years were usually matched with years of decline. Throughout two hundred years they have adapted to changes in taste, and services have survived, albeit in a more modest form than in the past. The coastline is as magnificent as ever and, as long as it attracts and thrills the public, then a cruise on a pleasure steamer will be the ultimate way in which to enjoy its many beauties.

Pleasure steamers were popular for providing the best way of seeing the glorious coastal scenery of Britain. They enabled passengers to relax in a deckchair or to have a meal while enjoying the view. Here, *Balmoral* is shown cruising in the Menai Strait in 2005.

PLEASURE STEAMERS AND THEIR OPERATORS

THAMES AND MEDWAY

Belle Steamers: *Clacton Belle, London Belle, Southwold Belle,Walton Belle, Woolwich Belle,Yarmouth Belle.*

General Steam Navigation Company: *Crested Eagle, Golden Eagle, Halcyon, Isle of Arran, Kingfisher, Laverock, Mavis, Oriole, Philomel, Queen of the Channel, Royal Eagle, Royal Daffodil, Royal Sovereign.*

New Medway Steam Packet Company: *Audrey, City of Rochester, Clacton Queen, Medway Queen, Princess of Wales, Queen of Kent, Queen of Thanet, Rochester Queen.*

New Palace Steamers: *Koh-i-noor, La Marguerite, Royal Sovereign.*

SOUTH COAST

British Railways: *Brading, Shanklin, Southsea.*

Cosens: *Albert Victor, Alexandra, Brodick Castle, Consul, Embassy, Empress, Emperor of India, Majestic, Monarch, Premier,Victoria.*

P. & A. Campbell: *Albion, Brighton Belle, Brighton Queen, Glen Rosa.*

Red Funnel: *Balmoral, Bournemouth Queen, Duchess of York, Gracie Fields, Her Majesty, Lorna Doone, Princess Elizabeth, Princess Helena, Princess Mary, Prince of Wales, Queen, Solent Queen, Stirling Castle,Vectis.*

Southern Railway: *Duchess of Albany, Freshwater, Ryde, Sandown,Whippingham.*

BRISTOL CHANNEL

Barry Railway: *Barry, Devonia, Gwalia,Westonia.*

P. & A. Campbell: *Albion, Bonnie Doon, Bristol Queen, Britannia, Cambria, Cardiff Queen, Devonia, Empress Queen, Glen Avon, Glen Gower, Glen Rosa, Glen Usk, Gwalia, Lady Ismay, Lady Margaret, Ravenswood,Waverley,Westward Ho.*

FIRTH OF CLYDE

Caledonian Steam Packet Company: *Caledonia, Duchess of Fife, Duchess of Hamilton, Duchess of Montrose, Glen Sannox, Jeanie Deans, King Edward, Maid of Argyll, Maid of the Loch, Marchioness of Breadalbane, Marchioness of Lorne, Mercury, Queen Mary II,Talisman,Waverley.*

David MacBrayne: *Chevalier, Columba, Fusilier, Gondolier, Grenadier, Iona, King George V, Pioneer.*

Glasgow & South Western Railway: *Atalanta, Glen Sannox, Heather Bell, Juno, Jupiter, Mars, Mercury.*

London & North Eastern Railway: *Jeanie Deans, Lucy Ashton, Prince Edward, Prince George, Princess May,Talisman.*